MY BOOK

MY ENGLISH ZONE

My picture or drawing

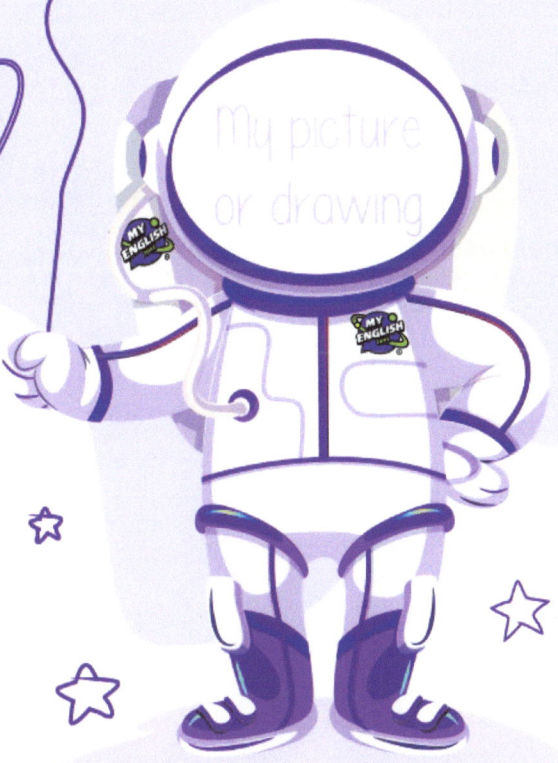

Published by UnilX Education

books@unilxeducation.com
USA +1 619 798 6274
MEX +52 6631030487

MyEnglishGameZone®, 2021 ©UnilX LLC, 2021

First Published 2021

Author: Patricia Armida Ávila Delfín
Editor: Sandra Rojas
Main Characters: My English Game Zone®
Cover and Complimentary Graphics: UnilX, Innovalingua Design Team and Freepik.com
Illustration, Design and Animation Leader: Rafael Orellana
Editorial Design: UNIGRÁPHICA, UnilX editorial team, Rafael Orellana

PROGRAM SYNOPSIS

The fundamental objective of **My English Zone The Book** is learning to communicate through interaction in the target language. The Theory of Language learning tells us that "language is a tool for communication and that students learn a language by using it to communicate."

You will find that **My English Zone The Book** is a series based on guided everyday communicative interaction. E.g. when students are faced with real life dialogs to find out the schedule of the week's exams or to describe a classmate by his/her physical appearance, among many other authentic situations. Guided dialogs provide opportunities for language learners to interact with each other or with native speakers while feeling comfortable doing so.

This series also acknowledges the role of grammar as that of great importance for our learners to reach higher levels of proficiency and introduces the basic structures from the start of the program.

My English Zone The Book also makes extensive use of authentic texts like: songs, jokes, rhymes, tongue twisters and popular children's stories. They will enrich the knowledge of culture through language.

As you can see, **My English Zone The Book** has a solid base on the most important methodologies necessary to enhance the learning of the second language in a dynamic and fun way.

Patricia Avila Delfin

SERIES FEATURES

- Each book with 15 units.
- Each unit has five lessons:

Book number	CEFR
1	Pre-A1
2	Pre-A1
3	A1.1
4	A1.2
5	A2.1
6	A2.1
7	A2.2
8	A2.2
9	B1.1
10	B1.2
11	B1.3
12	B1+

Lesson 1: Vocabulary
In this first lesson the vocabulary that will be used during the rest of the unit will be presented through clear images that represent each word.

Lesson 2: Dialogs
The dialogs will recap the vocabulary items from lesson one and use them in everyday real situations.

Lesson 3: Reading
The reading texts will go from original stories that take the ideas of the dialogs and complete them in a text to popular stories from children's literature.

Lesson 4: Writing
Prompted writing is used in the lower levels. It encourages students to use their imagination to come up with new and creative ideas for the text. In the higher levels, students will be asked to arrange the paragraphs or the missing sentences to complete the stories they read before.

Lesson 5: Language in Use
The last part of each unit, recaps the grammar structures seen, through the presentation of language in use of the four lessons before it. There are activities that will evaluate the knowledge acquired.

Vocabulary Learning

Vocabulary learning is central to language acquisition.

Specialists emphasize the need for a systematic and principled approach of vocabulary by the teacher and the learner. Teaching techniques and activities state that new words should not be learned by simple rote memorization.

It is important that new vocabulary items be presented in contexts rich enough to provide clues to meaning and that students be given multiple exposure to items they should learn.

Communicative Language Learning

Learning to communicate through interaction in the target language is the principal characteristic of the Communicative Language Teaching approach.

The The*ory of Language Learning states that:*
• *Langu*age is a tool for communication
• Students learn a language by using it to communicate

Integrated Skills Approach

The four basic skills in language teaching are: listening, speaking, reading , writing .

When we acquire a second language in a natural way the skills appear in that same order.

But why should we integrate the four skills when teaching the second language? If we are focused on teaching a realistic communication competence, the four skills must be developed in an integrated way .

Integrating the skills allows us to use more variety in the lessons because the range of activities will be ampler.

Spiral Learning

Learning should work like a game in a spiral, that gets a child interested while repeating and gradually increasing difficulty. It also gives students challenging activities and at the same time adds new skills.

The steps to achieve Spiral Learning are:
• Introduce new language. Move forward.
• Recap the important language learned so far.
• Add more language.
• Recap selected language: recent and earlier.
• Repeat the process.

Topic Based Approach

Topic based approach is student-centered. It helps with students' attention span.
It will hold students' interest from the start to the end of the lesson.

CONTENTS MAP

MY PLATFORM ACCESS

URL: _____

User name: _____

Password: _____

Ask your teacher or parents if you have a platform access.

Learn the activities

Unscramble the words. Match them with their images.

cguntit   _____.

entisnigl   _____.

gniroolc   _____.

gpnaist   _____.

plngayi   _____.

rtngwii   _____.

sgniing   _____.

Practice the dialogs

Is Andy playing?
-No, he isn't.
He's singing.

Is Sandy singing?
-No, she isn't.
She's pasting.

Is Lucy coloring?
-No, she isn't.
She's cutting.

Is Tony pasting?
-No, he isn't.
He's writing

Is Andy writing?
-No, he isn't.
He's singing.

Now you!

Is _____ _____?
No, he/she isn't.
He's / She's _____.

8

A busy day at school

It's very busy at school today.
Andy is not coloring; he's singing.
Lucy is not singing; she's cutting.
Tony is not listening; he's playing.
Sandy is not writing; she's pasting.
And Miss Patty is not playing;
she's listening to the class.
Yes, it is very busy at school today!

Choose the correct answer

Is Andy coloring?

❑ Yes, he is. ❑ No, he isn't.

Is Tony listening?

❑ Yes, he is. ❑ No, he isn't.

Is Andy singing?

❑ Yes, he is. ❑ No, he isn't.

Is Tony playing?

❑ Yes, he is. ❑ No, he isn't.

Is Lucy singing?

❑ Yes, she is. ❑ No, she isn't.

Is Sandy writing?

❑ Yes, she is. ❑ No, she isn't.

Is Lucy cutting?

❑ Yes, she is. ❑ No, she isn't.

Is Sandy pasting?

❑ Yes, she is. ❑ No, she isn't.

Complete the text with the words from the box below. You may write them in any order you wish and as many times as you wish.

At busy day at school

It's very busy at school today.
Andy is not _____ ; he's _____.
Lucy is not _____ ; she's _____.
Tony is not_____ ; he's _____.
Sandy is not _____ ; she's _____.
And Miss Patty is not _____ ; she's _____.
Yes, it is very busy at school today!

coloring • cutting •listening • pasting
playing • singing • writing

Write the words. Say them aloud

coloring	coloring
cutting	cutting
listening	listening
pasting	pasting
playing	playing
singing	singing
writing	writing

Present Progressive Tense.
The present progressive tense expresses a current action, an action in progress.
He is writing now.

We use the verb **BE** as a helping verb.

In sentences with HE, SHE, IT we use the verb **IS**.
He **is** singing now.

To make a question we put **IS** before the pronoun.
Is he coloring?

To make negative sentences we use **IS + NOT**
He **is not** (isn't) playing

Unscramble the sentences

____ ____ ____ ____
cutting   Lucy   is   ?

____ ____ ____ .
Tony   playing   is

____ ____ ____ ____
Is   pasting   Sandy   ?

____ ____ ____ .
isn't   coloring   Andy

____ ____ ____ .
reading   isn't   Tony

Answer the questions in the negative form

Is Andy coloring?
__, __ __ _____. .

Is Lucy cutting?
__, __ __ _____.

Is Tony listening?
__, __ __ _____.

Is Sandy pasting?
__, __ __ _____.

Is Lucy singing?
__, __ __ _____.

How well did you do in this unit?

_____

Write the CAN DO statement and assess yourself:

I can...

_____

_____

_____

_____

_____

_____

_____

Learn the food

Unscramble the words. Match them with their images.

aeerlc _____.

chcknei _____.

uiejc _____.

lkmi _____.

dlsaa _____.

wichdnsa _____.

eat _____.

retaw _____.

Practice the dialogs

What are you drinking?
-I am drinking water.
Great!

What are you eating?
-I am eating cereal.
Great!.

What are you drinking?
-I am drinking tea.
Great!

What are you eating?
-I am eating chicken.
Great!

What are you drinking?
-I am drinking juice.
Great!

What are you eating?
-I am eating salad.
Great!

What are you drinking?
-I am drinking milk.
Great!

Now you!

What are you
eating/drinking?
I am eating/drinking

_____.
Great!

At the school cafeteria

There is delicious lunch
at my school cafeteria every day.
Today I am eating a sandwich and drinking juice.
Sandy and Tony are eating salad and drinking tea.
Lucy and Andy are drinking water and eating chicken.
We are all drinking and eating delicious
lunch at the school cafeteria.

Choose true or false for each sentence

There isn't delicious lunch at my school cafeteria.
❏ True   ❏ False
I am eating salad.
❏ True   ❏ False
Sandy and Andy are drinking water.
❏ True   ❏ False
Lucy and Andy are eating chicken.
❏ True   ❏ False
We aren't drinking and eating delicious lunch at the school cafeteria.
❏ True   ❏ False

Choose the correct answer

Sandy is eating:
❏ salad   ❏ cereal
Tony is drinking:
❏ water   ❏ tea
Lucy is eating:
❏ chicken   ❏ sandwich
Andy is drinking:
❏ water   ❏ milk
I am drinking:
❏ water   ❏ juice
I am eating:
❏ sandwich   ❏ chicken

Complete the text with the words from the box below. You may write them in any order you wish.

At the school cafeteria

There is delicious lunch at my school cafeteria every day.
Today I am eating _____
and drinking _____.
Sandy and Tony are eating _____
and drinking _____.
Lucy and Andy are drinking _____
and eating _____.
We are all drinking and eating delicious lunch at the school cafeteria.

cereal • chicken • juice • milk
salad • sandwich • tea • water

Write the words. Say them aloud.

cereal   cereal
chicken   chicken
juice   juice
milk   milk
salad   salad
sandwich   sandwich
tea   tea
water   water

Present Progressive Tense
We use the present progressive tense to express an action that is taking place at this moment.

We form the Present Progressive tense with the verb BE+ ing at the end of the principal verb.
We **are** drink**ing** juice.
They **are** eat**ing** chicken.

Wh question:
What are you eating?
I am eating cereal.

Unscramble the sentences

_____ _____ _____ _____?
you / are / eating / what

_____ _____ _____ _____
eating / am / I / chicken

_____ _____ _____ _____?
drinking / you / are / what

_____ _____ _____ _____?
juice / we / drinking / are

_____ _____ _____ _____
drinking / milk / are / they

Put the name of the food under the correct column

drinking	eating
_____	_____
_____	_____
_____	_____
_____	_____

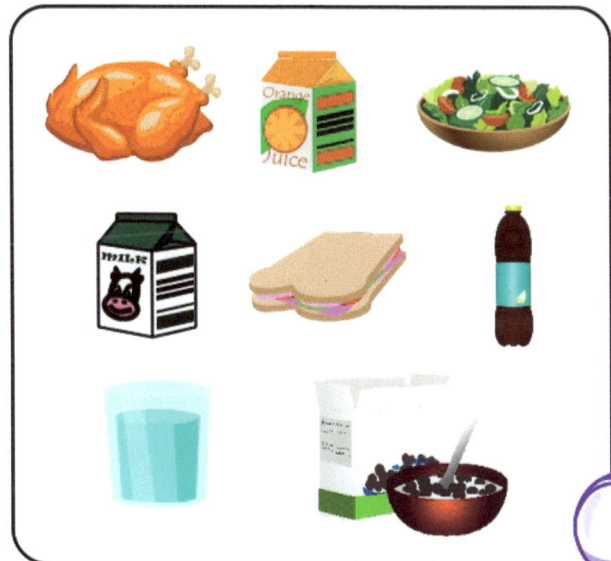

How well did you do in this unit?

Write the CAN DO statement and assess yourself:

I can...

Learn the activities at home

brushing

drinking

listening

writing

singing

eating

cooking

Practice the dialogs

What are you doing?
-I am brushing my teeth.
Ok!

What are you doing?
-I am writing a letter!
Ok!

What are you doing?
-I am cooking!
Ok!

What are you doing?
-I am eating.
Ok!

What are you doing?
-I am listening to music.
Ok!

What are you doing?
-I am drinking water!
Ok!

Now you!

What are you doing?
-I am _____.
Ok!

Busy at home

We are all busy at home today.
My father is cooking lunch and
my mother is drinking water in the yard.
My brother is eating a sandwich and
my sister is listening to music.
My grandmother is singing and
my grandfather is writing a letter.
And I am busy too. I am brushing my teeth.
It is a busy day at my home today!

Choose the correct answer

Father is:
- ❑ cooking
- ❑ listening to music
- ❑ drinking water

Mother is:
- ❑ eating
- ❑ drinking water
- ❑ cooking

Brother is :
- ❑ cooking
- ❑ drinking water
- ❑ eating

Sister is:
- ❑ listening to music
- ❑ cooking
- ❑ writing

Grandmother is:
- ❑ singing
- ❑ writing
- ❑ cooking

Grandfather is:
- ❑ drinking water
- ❑ singing
- ❑ writing

I am:
- ❑ brushing my teeth
- ❑ cooking
- ❑ singing

Complete the reading with the words from the box below

Busy at home

We are all busy at home today.
My father is _____ and my mother is _____ in the
yard. My brother is _____ and my sister is _____.
My grandmother is _____ and my grandfather is
_____

And I am busy too. I am _____.
It is a busy day at my home today!

brushing teeth • cooking lunch • drinking water
eating a sandwich • listening to music
singing songs • writing a letter

Write the words. Say them aloud.

brushing   brushing
cooking   cooking
drinking   drinking
eating   eating
listening   listening
singing   singing
writing   writing

> What are you **DOING?**
> Asks for an **action.**

> What are you **doing?**
> I am **eating** a sandwich.
>
> What is Lucy **doing?**
> She is **singing**.

What are you doing?
Match the sentence with the correct image

- I am brushing my teeth.

- I am cooking.

- I am drinking water.

- I am eating.

- I am listening to music.

- I am singing.

- I am writing.

How well did you do in this unit?

Write the CAN DO statement and assess yourself:

I can...

Learn the activities at home

playing
(instrument)

jumping

watching

cleaning

feeding

sleeping

resting

Find the home activities

P	B	P	O	J	K	A	I	F	B
W	X	M	R	P	N	Y	C	E	X
A	V	P	E	L	A	Z	L	E	B
T	X	O	S	A	S	J	E	D	R
C	W	V	T	Y	P	L	A	I	U
H	N	Y	I	I	X	Q	N	N	A
I	W	B	N	N	K	Q	I	G	S
N	B	K	G	G	Z	Q	N	D	G
G	C	R	V	M	P	A	G	P	S
G	N	I	P	E	E	L	S	C	V

CLEANING

FEEDING

JUMPING

PLAYING

RESTING

SLEEPING

WATCHING

Practice the dialogs

Is father feeding the dog?
-No, he isn't. He's feeding the cat.

Is mother playing the piano?
-No, she isn't. She's playing the guitar.

Is sister sleeping in the yard?
-No, she isn't.
She's sleeping in the bedroom.

Are grandma and grandpa watching videos?
-No, they aren't.
They are watching a movie.

Now you!

Is/Are_____?
No, _____.
_____.

A nice day at home

Today is a nice day at home.
What is my family doing? Well…
My father is feeding the cat.
My mother is playing the guitar.
My brother is resting in the TV room.
My sister is sleeping in the bedroom.
My grandma and grandpa are watching a movie.
My friends are jumping rope in the yard.
What am I doing? I am cleaning the room.
Yes, it is a nice day at home!

Circle ✔ if the sentence is true.
Circle ✘ if the sentence is false.

Mother is playing the piano.
✔   ✘

Father is feeding the cat.
✔   ✘

Brother is resting in the TV room.
✔   ✘

Sister is sleeping in the yard.
✔   ✘

Grandma and grandpa are watching videos.
✔   ✘

My friends are jumping rope on the street.
✔   ✘

I am cleaning the kitchen.
✔   ✘

Choose the correct answer

What is father doing?
❑ feeding the cat
❑ feeding the dog
What is mother doing?
❑ playing the piano
❑ playing the guitar
What is brother doing?
❑ resting in the TV room
❑ resting in the bedroom
What is sister doing?
❑ sleeping in the yard
❑ sleeping in the bedroom
What are grandma and grandpa doing?
❑ watching a movie
❑ watching videos

Complete the text with the words from the box below.
You may write them in any order you wish.

A nice day at home

Today is a nice day at home.
What is my family doing? Well...
My father is _____. My mother is _____.
My brother is _____. My sister is _____.
My grandma and grandpa are _____.
My friends are _____.
What am I doing? I am _____.
Yes, it is a nice day at home!

feeding the cat • playing the guitar • resting in the TV
room • sleeping in the bedroom • cleaning the room
watching a movie • jumping rope in the yard

Write the words. Say them aloud.

cleaning	cleaning
feeding	feeding
jumping	jumping
playing	playing
resting	resting
sleeping	sleeping
watching	watching

Present Progressive Tense
We make the negative form in the Present
Progressive Tense by adding NOT after the verb BE.

He is not cleaning the kitchen.

A short negative answer in the negative form is:
No, (comma) he isn't. (period)

The question
What are you doing?
Asks an action as an answer.
What are you doing?
I am playing the piano

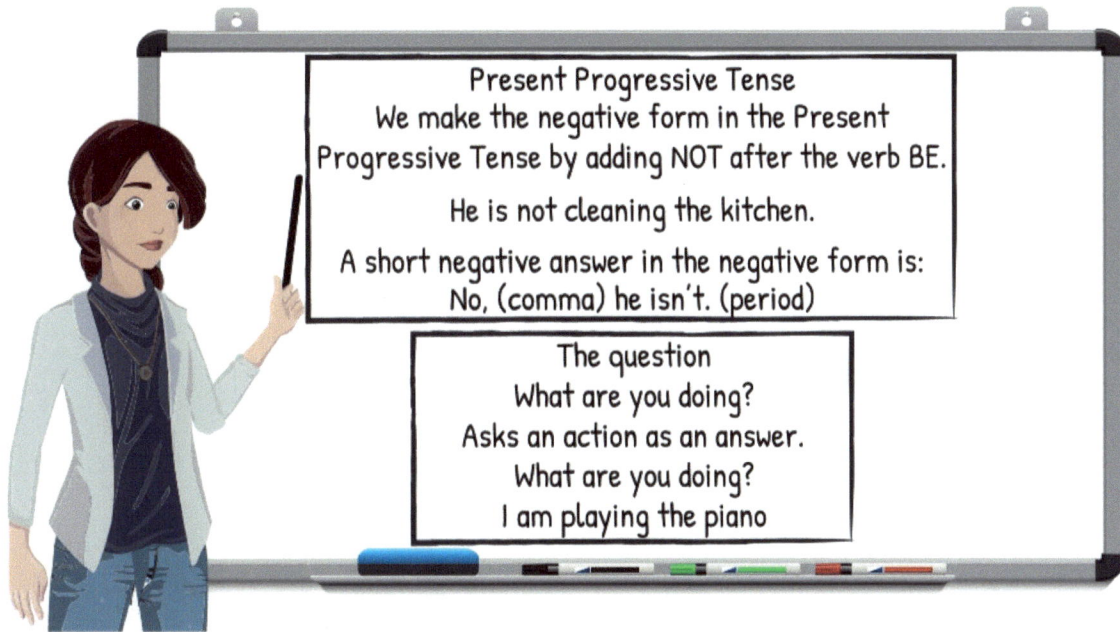

Choose the correct answer

Is father feeding the dog?
❑ No, he isn't.   ❑ No he isn't
❑ No, she isn't.

Is mother playing the piano?
❑ No she isn't   ❑ No, he isn't.
❑ No, she isn't.

Are you cleaning the kitchen?
❑ No, I'm not.   ❑ No, they aren't.
❑ No, he isn't.

Are grandma and grandpa
watching videos?
❑ No, they aren't
❑ No, we aren't ❑ No, she isn't.

Are your friends jumping rope
on the street?
❑ No, we aren't ❑ No, they aren't.
❑ No, I'm not.

Choose the correct verb

What _____ you doing?
❑ is   ❑ am   ❑ are

What _____ he doing?
❑ is ❑ am ❑ are

What _____ they doing?
❑ is ❑ am ❑ are

He _____ cleaning the room.
❑ am ❑ is ❑ are

I _____ playing the guitar.
❑ am ❑ is ❑ are

They _____ watching a movie.
❑ am ❑ is ❑ are

She _____ playing.
❑ am not ❑ isn't ❑ aren't

How well did you do in this unit?

Write the CAN DO statement and assess yourself:

I can...

Learn the activities at home

Unscramble the words

gniylap

_____

oomdbre

_____

slpngeei

_____

htrmbaoo

_____

aeitng

_____

ieatng

_____

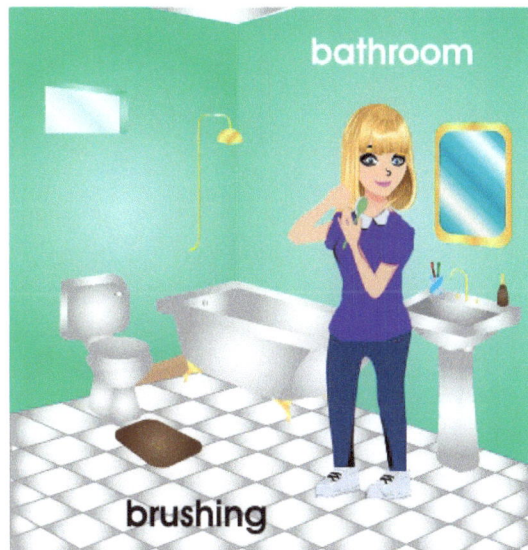

Practice the dialogs

Where is brother?
-He's in the living room.
What is he doing?
-He's watching his TV.

Where are you?
-I am in the yard.
What are you doing?
-I am playing.

Where is sister?
-She's in the bathroom.
What is she doing?
-She is brushing her hair.

Now you!

Where are/ is _____?

_____

What are/is _____?

_____

My happy family

My family is happy today.
My father is eating his lunch in the kitchen.
My brother is watching TV in the living room.
My sister is brushing her hair in the bathroom.
My mother is sleeping in her bedroom.
What am I doing? I am playing in the yard.
We are a happy family!

Circle ✔ if the sentence is true.
Circle ✘ if the sentence is false.

Circle the correct word
to complete the sentence

Father is eating lunch.
✔   ✘

Brother is watching TV.
✔   ✘

Sister is brushing her teeth.
✔   ✘

Mother is playing in the yard.
✔   ✘

I am sleeping in the bedroom.
✔   ✘

My father is _____.
◆ sleeping ◆ watching TV
◆ eating

My brother is _____.
◆ sleeping ◆ watching TV
◆ eating

My sister is _____.
◆ playing ◆ sleeping
◆ brushing

My mother is _____.
◆ playing ◆ sleeping
◆ brushing

I am _____.
◆ playing ◆ sleeping
◆ brushing

Complete the text with the words from the box below. You may write them in any order you wish.

My happy family

My family is happy today.
My father is _____ in the kitchen. My brother is _____ in the living room. My sister is _____ in the bathroom. My mother is _____ in her bedroom. What am I doing? I am _____ in the yard. We are a happy family!

sleeping • brushing hair • watching TV
eating lunch • playing

Write the words. Say them aloud

sleeping   sleeping

brushing   brushing

watching   watching

eating   eating

playing   playing

34

Possessive Adjectives
We use possessive adjectives to show **ownership** of something

Sandy is brushing **her** hair.
Tony is eating **his** sandwich.
Lucy and I are playing with **our** dog.
Grandma and grandpa are in **their** house.
You are cleaning **your** room.
I am playing **my** guitar.

Write the correct adjective from the box

I am playing in _____ house.
Lucy is brushing _____ hair.
Tony is eating _____ sandwich.
We are coloring in _____ books.
They are brushing _____ teeth.
You are sleeping in _____ bedroom.

my	its
your	our
his	their
her	

Circle the correct adjective

Andy is writing in ___ notebook.
◆ my ◆ your ◆ his
My friends are playing with ___ ball.
◆ his ◆ her ◆ their
Sandy is eating ___ pizza.
◆ her ◆ his ◆ my
I am resting in ___ room.
◆ our ◆ your ◆ my
We are listening to ___ teacher.
◆ our ◆ your ◆ their
You are brushing ___ hair.
◆ our ◆ your ◆ their

How well did you do in this unit?

Write the CAN DO statement and assess yourself:

I can...

ON THE MOVE!

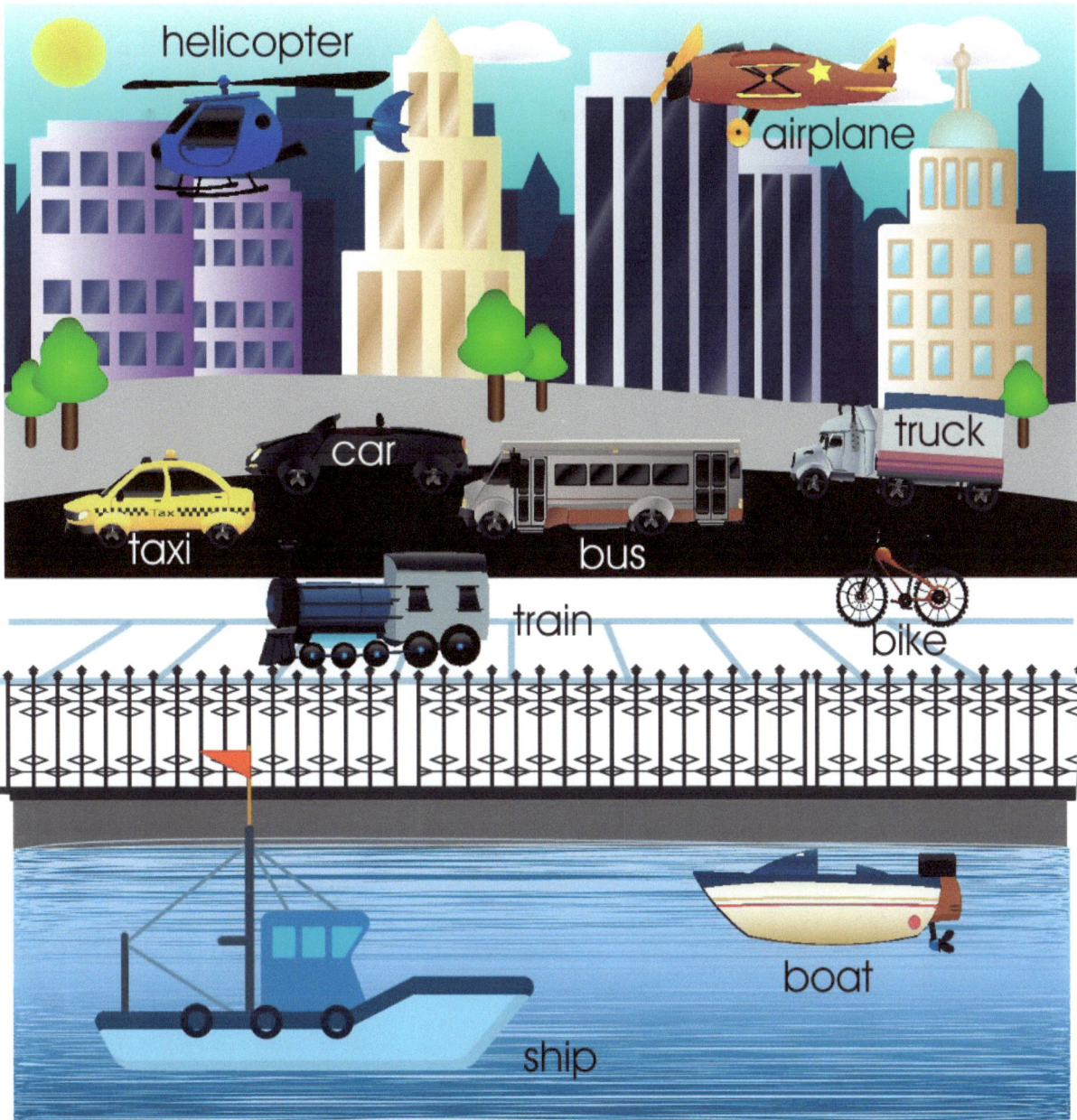

Unscramble the transportation word

aiaerpln	bcyclei
_____	_____
phsi	ianrt
_____	_____
aotb	krcut
_____	_____

37

Practice the dialogs

Guess what?
I can ride a bike!
- Really?
Sure, I can!

Guess what?
My grandma can fly a helicopter!
- Really?
Sure, she can!

Guess what?
My brother can drive a car!
- Really?
Sure, he can!

Guess what?
My sister can ride a motorcycle!
- Really?
Sure, she can!

Guess what?
My mom can drive a taxi!
- Really?
Sure, she can!

Tax

Guess what?
My cousins can sail a boat!
- Really?
Sure, they can!

Guess what?
My dad can drive a bus!
- Really?
Sure, he can!

Now you!

Guess what?
My _____ can
_____.
- Really?
Sure, _____ can!

On the move!

My family is sure on the move!
My dad can drive a bus and
my mother can drive a taxi.
My brother can drive a car and
my sister can ride a motorcycle.
My uncle can fly a plane and
my aunt can drive a truck.
My cousins can sail a boat.
My grandma can fly a helicopter and
my grandpa can run a train.
And guess what? I can ride a bike.
We are all sure on the move!

Circle ✔ if the sentence is true.
Circle ✘ if the sentence is false.

My aunt can fly a plane.
✔ ✘

My brother can drive a car.
✔ ✘

My grandma can run a train.
✔ ✘

My cousins can sail a boat.
✔ ✘

My mom can ride a motorcycle.
✔ ✘

My dad can fly a helicopter.
✔ ✘

My uncle can fly a plane.
✔ ✘

I can ride a bike.
✔ ✘

Choose the correct answer

My mom can drive a:

☐ bus ☐ taxi ☐ car

My sister can ride a:

☐ bicycle ☐ motorcycle ☐ train

My grandma can fly a:

☐ helicopter ☐ plane ☐ balloon

My cousins can sail a:

☐ ship ☐ boat ☐ jet ski

I can ride:

☐ bicycle ☐ motorcycle ☐ train

Complete the text with the words from the box below. You may write them in any order you wish.

On the move !

My family is sure on the move!
My dad can _____
and my mother can _____. My brother can
_____
and my sister can _____. My uncle can
_____
and my aunt can _____.
My cousins can _____.
My grandma can _____
and my grandpa can _____. And guess what?
I can _____.

We are all sure on the move!

fly an airplane • ride a bicycle • sail a boat •
drive a bus • drive a car • fly a helicopter
ride a motorcycle • drive a taxi • run a train • drive a truck

Write the words. Say them aloud.

airplane	helicopter
bicycle	motorcycle
boat	taxi
bus	train
car	truck

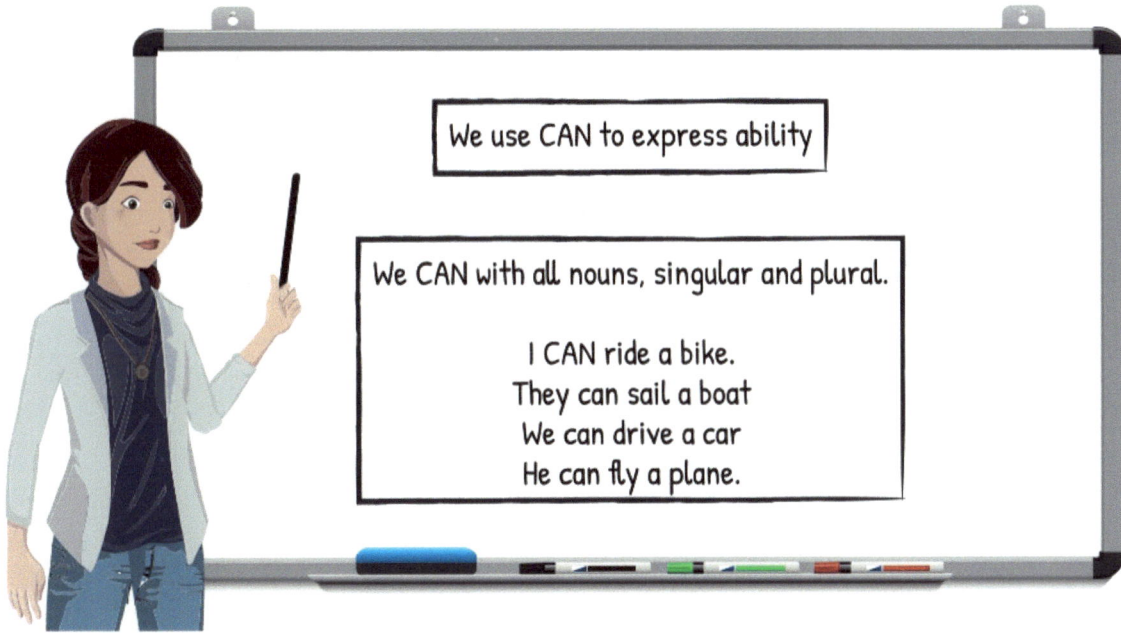

We use CAN to express ability

We CAN with all nouns, singular and plural.

I CAN ride a bike.
They can sail a boat
We can drive a car
He can fly a plane.

Unscramble the sentences

_____ ____ _____ ____ _____.
dad / a / bus / drive / can

_____ ____ _____ ____ _____.
fly / plane / can / a / uncle

_____ ____ _____ ____ _____.
fly / helicopter / grandma / can / a

_____ ____ _____ ____ _____.
ride / a / motorcycle / can / sister

_____ ____ _____ ____ _____.
sail / boat / a / cousins / can

Match the sentence halves to complete the sentences

My brother …   can drive a car.

My grandma …   can fly a plane.

My cousins …   can sail a boat.

My uncle …   fly a helicopter.

I can …   ride a bike.

How well did you do in this unit?

Write the CAN DO statement and assess yourself:

I can...

Learn the means of animals

dolphin	eagle	lion
swim	fly	roar

horse	dog
run	bark

Find the animal words

D	D	D	O	L	P	H	I	N	F
G	O	X	N	F	S	W	I	M	W
V	G	H	B	M	H	G	U	J	L
M	P	E	A	G	L	E	S	W	I
A	T	E	R	G	E	Q	C	N	O
S	E	D	K	F	O	Q	D	D	N
P	D	R	F	H	C	L	P	G	X
L	G	O	L	R	U	N	X	Q	K
B	L	A	Y	T	H	O	R	S	E
H	I	R	M	G	B	O	C	T	W

DOLPHIN
EAGLE
LION
HORSE
DOG

Practice the dialogs

Can a dolphin swim?
-Yes, it can. But it can't fly.

Can a horse run?
-Yes, it can. But it can't fly.

Can a dog bark?
-Yes, it can. But it can't roar.

Can a lion roar?
-Yes, it can. But it can't bark.

Can an eagle fly?
-Yes, it can. But it can't swim

Now you!

Can a _____ _____?
Yes, it can.
But it can't _____

Fantastic animals!

Animals are fantastic,
they can do many things!
An eagle can fly but it can't swim.
A dolphin can swim but it can't run.
A horse can run but it can't roar.
A lion can roar but it can't bark.
A dog can bark but it can't fly,
but I love dogs anyway.

Circle ✔ if the sentence is true.
Circle ✘ if the sentence is false.

Choose the correct answer

A dolphin can´t run
✔   ✘

A lion can swim
✔   ✘

A dog can´t fly
✔   ✘

A eagle can bark
✔   ✘

A horse can´t run
✔   ✘

A dolphin can swim
✔   ✘

A dolphin can:
❑ run   ❑ swim   ❑ fly

A dog can:
❑ fly   ❑ roar   ❑ bark

A eagle can:
❑ swim   ❑ roar   ❑ fly

A lion can:
❑ roar   ❑ swim   ❑ bark

A horse can:
❑ run   ❑ fly   ❑ bark

45

Complete the text with the words from the box below.
You may write them in any order you wish.

Fantastic animals

Animals are fantastic, they can do many things!

A eagle can _____ but it can´t _____.

A dolphin can _____ but it can´t _____.

A horse can _____ but it can´t _____.

A lion can _____ but it can´t _____.

A dog can _____ but it can´t _____.

But I love dogs anyway.

bark • run • roar • fly • swim

Write the words. Say them aloud.

bark	dolphin
run	eagle
roar	lion
fly	horse
swim	dog

We use **CAN** to express ability
We use **CAN** with all nouns, singular and plural.

For interrogative sentences we use **CAN** before the subject.
Can a dolphin swim?
For negative sentences we use CAN +NOT= CAN'T
A dolphin **can't** fly.

Complete the sentences

A dog _____ roar.
• can   • can't
An eagle _____ fly.
• can   • can't
A horse _____ run.
• can   • can't
A dolphin _____ fly.
• can   • can't
A lion _____ bark.
• can   • can't

Unscramble the sentences

_____ _____ ___ _____ _____
run / dolphin / a / can / ?

_____ _____ ___ _____ _____
? / dog / a / can / fly

_____ _____ ___ _____ _____
an / can / ? / swim / eagle

_____ _____ ___ _____ _____
roar / ? / horse / can / a

_____ _____ ___ _____ _____
lion / a / ? / can / bark

How well did you do in this unit?

Write the CAN DO statement and assess yourself:

I can...

Learn the five senses

taste   smell   see   touch   hear

My five senses

eyes   ears   nose   hands   tongue

Match the 5 senses

see *

touch*

smell*

hear*

taste*

49

Practice the dialogs

Can you see with your ears?
-Of course not, silly!
-I can see with my eyes.
Oh, that's right!

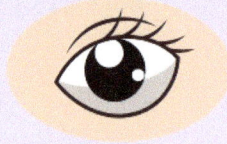

Can you taste with your hands?
-Of course not, silly!
-I can taste with my tongue.
Oh, that's right!

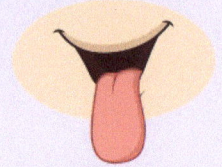

Can you hear with your nose?
-Of course not, silly!
-I can hear with my ears.
Oh, that's right!

Can you smell with your eyes?
-Of course not, silly!
-I can smell with my nose.
Oh, that's right!

Can you touch with your tongue?
-Of course not, silly!
-I can touch with my hands.
Oh, that's right!

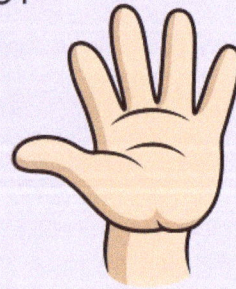

Now you!

Can you _____ with
your _____?
-Of course not, silly!
-I can _____ with my _____.
Oh, that's right!

Our incredible Five Senses

There are five incredible 5 senses in our bodies.
We can do many things with our senses.
We can see with our eyes.
We can hear with our ears.
We can smell with our nose.
We can touch with our hands.
We can taste with our tongue.
Yes, our senses are incredible!

Circle ✔ if the sentence is true.
Circle ✘ if the sentence is false.

Complete the sentences

We can see with our tongue.
✔ True ✘ False

We can taste with our hands.
✔ True ✘ False

We can touch with our nose.
✔ True ✘ False

We can hear with our ears.
✔ True ✘ False

We can smell with our nose.
✔ True ✘ False

I can see with my
_____.

I can hear with my
_____.

I can smell with my
_____.

I can touch with my
_____.

I can taste with my
_____.

Complete the text with the words from the box below. You may write them in any order you wish.

Our incredible five senses

There are five incredible senses in our bodies.
We can do many things with our senses.
We can see with our _____ but we can´t see with our _____.
We can taste with our _____ but we can´t taste with our _____.
We can hear with our _____ but we can´t hear with our _____.
We can touch with our _____ but we can´t touch with our _____.
We can smell with our _____ but we can´t smell with our _____.

Yes, our senses are incredible!

---

eyes (x2) • ears (x2) • nose (x2)
hands (x2) • tongue (x2)

Write the words. Say them aloud

ears	see
eyes	smell
hands	taste
hear	tongue
nose	touch

We use **CAN** to express ability
I **CAN** smell with my nose.

For negative sentences we use CAN+NOT = CAN'T
I can't smell with my eyes

Unscramble the sentences

_____ _____ _____ _____ _____ _____.
can't my smell with I ears

_____ _____ _____ _____ _____ _____.
ears my with hear can I

_____ _____ _____ _____ _____ _____.
I touch my can with hands

_____ _____ _____ _____ _____ _____.
nose with can't I see my

_____ _____ _____ _____ _____ _____.
taste can't with eyes my I

Answer the questions

Can you see with your nose?

No,_____

Can you smell with your eyes?

No,_____

Can you touch with your ears?

No, _____

Can you hear with your tongue?

No, _____

How well did you do in this unit?

Write the CAN DO statement and assess yourself:

I can...

Learn the verbs

sleep

get up

wash

watch

drink

clean

go

feed

play

eat

Practice the dialogs

I wash my hands
in the morning.
-Really? I wash my face
in the morning.

I drink juice in the morning.
-Really? I drink milk
in the morning.

I go to school
with my brother.
- Really? I go to
school with my sister.

I play tennis after school.
- Really? I play soccer
after school.

I eat lunch in the school yard.
- Really? I eat lunch in the
school cafeteria.

I feed my cat every day.
- Really? I feed
my dog every day.

I clean the kitchen
every afternoon.
- Really? I clean
my room every afternoon.

Now you!

I _____.

Really? I _____.

This is my day

I get up at 7 o'clock, and then I wash my face.
After that I drink milk and I go to school.
At school I eat lunch in the cafeteria.
After school I play soccer.
At home again, I feed the dog; of course,
I clean my room and then I watch TV.
Finally I sleep with my sister at 8 o'clock.
This is my day… every day!

Answer true or false

I get up at 7 o'clock.
❏ true   ❏ false
I drink juice.
❏ true   ❏ false
I wash my hands.
❏ true   ❏ false
I eat lunch in the cafeteria.
❏ true   ❏ false
I play soccer.
❏ true   ❏ false
I feed the cat.
❏ true   ❏ false
I clean the kitchen.
❏ true   ❏ false
I watch TV.
❏ true   ❏ false

Choose the correct answer

I get up at _____ .
❏ seven o'clock
❏ eight o'clock
❏ six o'clock
I feed the _____ .
❏ cat
❏ dog
❏ hamster
I play _____ after school.
❏ tennis
❏ basketball
❏ soccer
I sleep with my_____ .
❏ mother
❏ brother
❏ sister

Complete the text with words from the box below. Choose the one that fits you best.

This is my day

I get up at _____, and then I wash _____. After that I drink _____ and I go to school with _____. At school I eat lunch in the _____. After school I play _____. At home again, I feed the _____; of course, I clean my _____ and then I watch _____. Finally I sleep with my _____ at 8 o'clock.
This is my day… every day!

7 o'clock • 6 o'clock • cafeteria • yard • dog
cat • face • hand • milk • juice • room • kitchen
sister • brother • soccer • tennis • TV • videos

Write the words. Say them aloud.

clean   go

drink   play

eat   sleep

feed   wash

get up   watch

Present Simple Tense
We can express **habits**, **customs** and **routines**
with the Present Simple Tense.

In the affirmative the verb has no change.
We use the verb with no change with:
I, you, we, they.
I **go** to school every day.
You **go** to school every day.
We **go** to school every day.
They **go** to school every day.

Choose the correct verb

I _____ at 7 o'clock.
▶ get up ▶ drink
You _____ my face.
▶ brush ▶ wash
We _____ milk.
▶ go ▶ drink
They _____ to school.
▶ go ▶ eat
I _____ lunch.
▶ play ▶ eat
You _____ soccer.
▶ go ▶ play
We _____ the dog.
▶ feed ▶ eat

Write the correct verb

I _____ my face.
I _____ to school.
I _____ soccer.
I _____ the dog.
I _____ my room.
I _____ with my sister.
I _____ milk.
I _____ lunch.

clean	drink	eat
feed	go	play
sleep	wash	

How well did you do
in this unit?

Write the CAN DO statement and assess yourself:

I can...

Learn the community helpers

doctor

farmer

police officer

firefighter

pilot

teacher

makes people better

grows food

helps people

fights fires

flies planes

teaches children

Practice the dialogs

Look! A firefighter fights fires!
- Really? That's awesome!

Look! A farmer grows food!
-Really? That's super!

Look! A police officer helps people!
-Really? That's incredible!

Look! a teacher teaches children!
-Really? That's great!

Look! A doctor makes people feel better!
-Really? That's fantastic!

Look! A pilot flies planes!
-Really? That's cool!

Now you!

Look! A _____ _____ _____ !
- Really? That's cool!

Awesome people !

Today we are reading about awesome
people, community helpers!
We are reading that a doctor
makes people feel better.
A firefighter fights fires and a police officer
helps people, isn't that awesome?
A farmer grows food, like corn.
A teacher, like Miss Patty teaches children.
And a pilot flies planes, so cool!
Yes, community helpers are awesome people!

Circle ✔ if the sentence is true.
Circle ✘ if the sentence is false.

A teacher fights fires.
✔   ✘

A pilot flies planes.
✔   ✘

A police officer teaches
children.
✔   ✘

A farmer grows food.
✔   ✘

A doctor makes people feel
better.
✔   ✘

Choose the correct answer

A teacher _____ children.
❑ teaches ❑ fights ❑ flies

A pilot _____ planes.
❑ fights   ❑ helps ❑ flies

A police officer _____ people.
❑ teaches ❑ flies ❑ helps

A farmer _____ food.
❑ flies   ❑ grows ❑ teaches

A doctor _____ people feel
better.
❑ makes ❑ fights ❑ teaches

Complete the text with the following phrases in any order you like

Awesome people

Today we are reading about awesome people, community helpers!

We are reading that _____.

A _____ and a _____, isn't that awesome?

A _____ . A _____ . And a _____, so cool!

Yes, community helpers are awesome people!

doctor makes people better • farmer grows food
firefighter fights fires • pilot flies planes •
police officer helps people • teacher teaches children

Write the words. Say them aloud.

doctor	fight
farmer	fly
firefighter	grow
pilot	help
police officer	make
teacher	teach

Present Simple Tense
We can express **habits**, **customs** and **routines**
with the Present Simple Tense.

In the third person singular we add an "S" at the end of
the verb.
A police officer helps people.
We add an "S" to affirmative sentences with HE, SHE, IT.
He **eats** lunch.
She **plays** soccer.
It **runs** fast.

Write the correct form of the verb

A doctor _____ people feel better.

A teacher _____ children.

A farmer _____ food.

A pilot _____ planes.

A police officer _____ people.

A firefighter _____ fires.

Unscramble the sentences

__ _____ _____ _____.
a / teaches / children/ teacher

__ _____ _____ _____.
firefighter/ fires/ a/ fights

__ _____ _____ _____ _____.
a/helps/people/police/officer

__ _____ _____ _____.
grows/ food/ farmer/ a

__ _____ _____ _____.
flies / a / pilot / planes

65

How well did you do in this unit?

Write the CAN DO statement and assess yourself:

I can...

Learn the healthy habits

brush	brush	wash	wash

toothpaste			

toothbrush	brush	soap	shampoo

Unscramble the words. Match them with their picture.

aops

_____

ooamphs

_____

eaoottthsp

_____

tthbrshoou

_____

hswa

_____

ubhrs

_____

Practice the dialogs

Do you use soap every day?
-Yes, I do.
Why do you do that?
-Because it's a healthy habit.

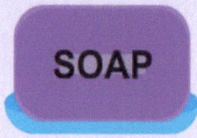

SOAP

Do you wash your hands every day?
-Yes, I do.
Why do you do that?
-Because it's a healthy habit

Do you use shampoo every day?
-Yes, I do.
Why do you do that?
-Because it's a healthy habit.

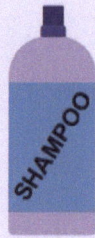

SHAMPOO

Do you wash your hair every day?
-Yes, I do.
Why do you do that?
-Because it's a healthy habit.

Do you use toothpaste every day?
-Yes, I do.
Why do you do that?
-Because it's a healthy habit.

TOOTHPASTE

Do you use a toothbrush every day?
-Yes, I do.
Why do you do that?
-Because it's a healthy habit.

Now you!

Do you use a _____ every day?
-Yes, I do.
Why do you do that?
-Because it's a healthy habit.

Healthy habits

Do you know what healthy habits are?
I DO!
Healthy habits are things like:
Using a toothbrush and toothpaste
to have strong teeth to chew .
Using shampoo to wash our hair
and a comb to comb it through.
Using soap to wash our hands and body too.
Why do we do that?
Because healthy habits are good for you!

Circle ✔ if the sentence is true.
Circle ✘ if the sentence is false.

Complete the sentences

We wash our hands with shampoo.
✔ ✘

We brush our teeth with a comb.
✔ ✘

We wash our hands with soap.
✔ ✘

We comb our hair with a comb.
✔ ✘

We brush our teeth with toothpaste.
✔ ✘

We wash our hands with
_____.

We brush our teeth with
_____.

We comb our hair with
_____.

We wash our hair with
_____.

Complete the text with the words and phrases from the box in any order you like.

Healthy habits

Do you know what healthy habits are?
I DO!
Healthy habits are things like:

Using _____.
Using _____.
Using_____.

Why do we do that?
Because healthy habits are good for you!

- a toothbrush and toothpaste to have strong teeth to chew
- shampoo to wash our hair and a comb to comb it through
- soap to wash our hands and body too

Write the words. Say them aloud.

soap   soap
shampoo   shampoo
toothpaste   toothpaste
toothbrush   toothbrush
wash   wash
brush   brush
comb   comb

We the auxiliary verb DO, to ask questions in the
Present Simple Tense.

We use DO before the nouns:
I – YOU – WE – THEY
Do I use toothpaste every day?
Do you comb your hair every day?
Do they wash their hands every day?
Do we comb our hair every day?

Write the corresponding short answer to the following questions

Do they brush their hair every day?

_____

Do you brush your teeth every day?

_____

Do you and your sister shampoo
your hair every day?

_____

Do I wash my hands every day?

_____

Yes, they do.   Yes, I do.
Yes, we do.   Yes, you do.

Unscramble the sentences

____ ____ ____ ____

____ ____ .

?/ you/ comb/ your/ do/ hair

____ ____ ____ ____

____ ____ .

toothbrush/ use/ you/ do/ a/ ?

____ ____ ____ ____

____ .

Use/ you/ toothpaste/ do/ ?

____ ____ ____ ____

____ ____ .

you/ your/ ?/ do/ hands/ wash

How well did you do in this unit?

Write the CAN DO statement and assess yourself:

I can...

Learn the animals and what they do

duck

snake

tiger

fly

bird

slither   run

bear

sing

climb

Unscramble the words. Match with the picture.

raeb

_____

ckud

_____

trieg

_____

dbir

_____

eskna

_____

Practice the dialogs

Look at that snake!
-Does the snake slither?
Yes, it does. It slithers all day.

Look at that bird!
-Does the bird sing?
Yes, it does. It sings all the time.

Look at that tiger!
-Does the tiger run?
Yes, it does. It runs very fast.

Look at that duck!
-Does the duck fly?
Yes, it does. It flies very high.

Look at that bear!
-Does the bear climb?
Yes, it does. It climbs up trees.

Now you!

Look at that _____!
-Does the _____ _____?
Yes, it does. It _____.

Animal kingdom

Look at the amazing animals
and what they do all day long!
A snake slithers all day.
The bird sings all the time.
The tiger runs very fast.
The duck flies very high
and that bear climbs up trees.
They are all amazing animals
of the Animal Kingdom!

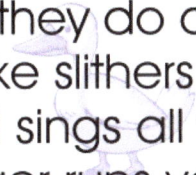

Circle ✔ if the sentence is true.
Circle ✘ if the sentence is false.

Complete the sentences

A snake slithers all day.
  ✔ True ✘ False

A bear sings all the time.
  ✔ True ✘ False

A duck flies very high.
  ✔ True ✘ False

A tiger runs very fast.
  ✔ True ✘ False

A bird climbs up trees.
  ✔ True ✘ False

Does the _____ run very fast?
Yes it does.

Does the _____ sing all the
time?
Yes, it does.

Does the _____ slither all day?
Yes, it does.

Does the _____ fly very high?
Yes, it does.

Complete the text with the words and phrases from the box below in any order you like.

Animal kingdom

Look at the amazing animals and what they do all day long!

A _____ _____. The _____ _____.

The _____ _____. The _____ _____ and that _____ _____.

They are all amazing animals of the Animal Kingdom!

bird • bear • tiger • snake • duck
sings all the time • climbs up trees • runs very fast
slithers all day • flies very high

Write the words. Say them aloud.

snake	slither
bird	sing
tiger	run
duck	fly
bear	climb

We the auxiliary verb DOES, to ask questions in the Present Simple Tense.

We use DOES before the nouns:
HE—SHE-- IT

Does the tiger run very fast?
Does she sing in festivals?
Does he fly kites?

Unscramble the sentences

_____ _____ _____ _____ _____

slither / snake / the /does / ?

_____ _____ _____ _____ _____

does / bird / the / sing / ?

_____ _____ _____ _____ _____

? / does / duck / the / fly

_____ _____ _____ _____ _____

climb / bear / the / does / ?

_____ _____ _____ _____ _____

? / the / run / tiger / does

Write the corresponding short answer to the following questions

Does the bear climb trees?
_____

Does your sister like dogs?
_____

Does your father run very fast?
_____

Does the bird sing all day?
_____

Does Sandy swim every day?
_____

Yes, he does.
Yes, she does.
Yes, it does.

How well did you do in this unit?

☆☆☆

_____

Write the CAN DO statement and assess yourself:

I can...

Learn the animals and what they do

wolf

bee

rabbit

monkey

howl

work

hop

climb

fish

swim

Unscramble the words. Match them with their picture.

aitbbr

_____

fwlo

_____

eeb

_____

yeomkn

_____

hsfi

_____

Practice the dialogs

Do rabbits swim?
No, they don't. They hop.

Does a wolf sing?
No, it doesn't. It howls.

Do bees climb?
No, they don't. They work.

Does a monkey howl?
No, it doesn't. It climbs.

Do fish hop?
No, they don't. They swim.

Now you!

Do _____ _____?
No, they don't. They _____.

At the zoo!

Look at all these wonderful animals,
and the amazing things they do.
Rabbits hop but they don't swim.
A wolf howls but it doesn't sing.
Bees work but they don't climb.
A monkey climbs but it doesn't howl.
Fish swim but they don't hop.
Yes, they are wonderful animals and
the things they do are amazing!

Circle ✔ if the sentence is true.
Circle ✘ if the sentence is false.

Choose the correct negative
to complete the sentence

Rabbits don't hop.

✔   ✘

A wolf doesn't sing.

✔   ✘

Bees don't work.

✔   ✘

A monkey doesn't climb.

✔   ✘

Fish don't hop.

✔   ✘

Rabbits _____ swim.
❏ don't ❏ doesn't

A wolf _____ sing.
❏ don't ❏ doesn't

Bees _____ climb.
❏ don't ❏ doesn't

A monkey _____ work.
❏ don't ❏ doesn't

Fish _____ hop.
❏ don't ❏ doesn't

Complete the text with the following words and phrases from the box below in any order you wish.

At the zoo!

Look at all these wonderful animals, and the amazing things they do.
Rabbits _____ but they don't _____ . A wolf _____ but it doesn't _____ . Bees _____ but they don't _____ . A monkey _____ but it doesn't _____ . Fish _____ but they don't _____ .
Yes, they are wonderful animals and the things they do are amazing!

hop   (x2) • howl (x2) • work (x2) • climb (x2)
swim (x2)

Write the words. Say them aloud.

bee   monkey

climb   rabbit

fish   swim

hop   wolf

howl   work

We use the auxiliary verb **DO+NOT, DOES+NOT** to make negative sentences in the Present Simple Tense.

We use **DON'T** with:
I – YOU – WE – THEY

We use **DOESN'T** with:
HE—SHE—IT

I **don't** swim.
You **don't** sing.
We **don't** run.
They **don't** climb.

He **doesn't** sing.
She **doesn't** swim.
It **doesn't** hop.

Write the corresponding negative form to complete the sentences

Rabbits_____ swim.

A wolf _____ sing.

Bees _____ climb.

A monkey _____ howl.

Fish _____ hop.

don't / doesn't

Complete the answers

Do rabbits swim?
No, they _____. They _____.

Does a wolf sing?
No, it _____. It _____.

Do bees climb?
No, they _____. They _____.

Does a monkey howl?
No, it _____. It _____.

Do fish hop?
No, they _____. They _____.

How well did you do in this unit?

Write the CAN DO statement and assess yourself:

I can...

Learn the buildings in town

school   hospital   fire station

farm   police station   airport

Find the names of the buildings

X	P	A	U	E	Q	S	E	H	B	H	B	J	W	O
X	H	I	S	J	J	W	W	L	W	X	O	V	M	O
K	C	R	A	D	R	G	O	D	G	W	P	Q	P	P
L	P	P	Y	M	X	V	I	L	O	O	H	C	S	I
H	R	O	K	F	Y	P	S	C	W	B	T	U	U	Z
S	Z	R	D	F	Y	P	Y	I	E	D	I	A	B	D
S	B	T	Y	Q	H	O	S	P	I	T	A	L	Y	Y
G	K	P	O	L	I	C	E	S	T	A	T	I	O	N
L	J	F	I	R	E	S	T	A	T	I	O	N	O	I
W	I	F	V	G	K	W	L	X	M	R	A	F	P	Z

POLICE STATION   SCHOOL
FIRE STATION   AIRPORT
HOSPITAL   FARM

85

Practice the dialogs

Who is she?
-She's a doctor.
Where does she work?
-She works in a hospital.
What does she do?
-She makes people feel better.

Who is he?
-He's a pilot.
Where does he work?
-He works in an airport.
What does he do?
-He flies planes.

Who is she?
-She's a firefighter.
Where does she work?
-She works in a fire station.
What does she do?
-She fights fires.

Who are they?
-They are farmers.
Where do they work?
-They work in a farm.
What do they do?
-They grow food.

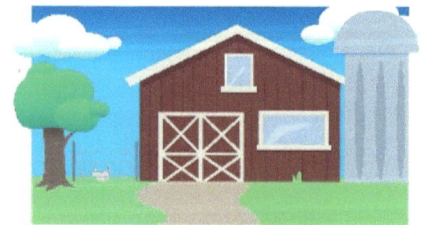

Who are they?
-They are teachers.
Where do they work?
-They work in a school.
What do they do?
-They teach children.

People that help us

There are people that help us every day.
They work very hard in different places in the city.
Doctors work in hospitals and teachers work in schools.
Firefighters work in fire stations and police officers work in police stations.
Pilots work in airports and farmers work in farms.
Thank you for all the work you do!

Who works there?

Who works in a hospital?
❑ doctor ❑ teacher ❑farmer

Who works in a school?
❑teacher ❑ farmer ❑ doctor

Who works in a police station?
❑pilot ❑police officer ❑doctor

Who works in a farm?
❑doctor ❑police officer ❑farmer

Who works in a fire station?
❑pilot ❑teacher ❑firefighter

Who works in an airport?
❑pilot ❑teacher ❑firefighter

Where do community helpers work?

Doctors work in _____
❑ schools ❑ fire stations ❑ hospitals

Teachers work in _____
❑ schools ❑ fire stations ❑ hospitals

Firefighters work in _____
❑ schools ❑ fire stations ❑ hospitals

Police officers work in _____
❑ police stations ❑ farms ❑ airports

Farmers work in_____
❑ police stations ❑ farms ❑ airports

Complete the text with the words and phrases from the box below in any order you like.

> ## People that help us
>
> There are people that help us every day. They work very hard in different places in the city.
>
> _____ work in _____ and _____ work in _____ .
> _____ work in _____ and _____ work in _____ .
> _____ work in _____ and _____ work in _____ .
>
> Thank you for all the work you do!

> doctors • teachers • pilots • farmers • police officers
> firefighters • hospitals • schools • airports • farms
> police stations • fire stations

Write the words. Say them aloud

> police station police station
> fire station fire station
> hospital hospital
> school school
> airport airport
> farm farm

WH questions in the Present Simple Tense

We make the Wh questions in the Present Simple:
WH word+ do/does+ subject+ verb + complement
Where do doctors work?
What do farmers do?
Where does a teacher work?
What does a teacher do?

Answer with complete sentences

Who works in a farm?

_____

Where do teachers work?

_____

Where does a pilot work?

_____

What does a doctor do?

_____

What do police officers do?

_____

Answer the questions

Who _____ in a hospital?
❑ work   ❑ works
Where _____ a doctor work?
❑ do   ❑ does
What does a doctor _____ ?
❑ do   ❑ does
Where _____ pilots work?
❑ do   ❑ does
What do pilots _____?
❑ do   ❑ does
Who _____ in a school?
❑ work   ❑ works
Where _____ a teacher work ?
❑ do   ❑ does
Where _____ teachers work ?
❑ do   ❑ does

How well did you do in this unit?

Write the CAN DO statement and assess yourself:

I can...

Vocabulary

USA
English

England
English

France
French

Mexico
Spanish

Japan
Japanese

Practice the dialogs

Hello! My name is Harry.
I am from England.
I speak English.

Konnichiwa!
Her name is Akiko.
She is from Japan.
She speaks Japanese.

Hi! His name is Tom.
He is from the USA.
He speaks English.

Hola! Our names
are Jose and Rosa.
We are from Mexico.
We speak Spanish.

Bonjour! Their names are
Michelle and Antoine.
They are from France.
They speak French.

Now you!

What _____ _____ name ?
_____ _____ ___ _____ .
Where _____ _____ _____ ?

_____ ___ from _____ .
What language _____
_____ speak?
_____ _____ _____ .

Friends from all around the world

We are friends from all over the world
and we speak different languages.
Harry is from England, he speaks English.
Tom is from the USA and he also speaks English.
Michelle and Antoine are from France,
they speak French.
Akiko is from Japan,
she speaks Japanese.
Jose and Rosa are from Mexico,
they speak Spanish.
Where are you from? What language do you speak?

Where are they from?

Where is Akiko from?
❑ Japan ❑ Mexico ❑ USA

Where is Tom From?
❑ England ❑ USA ❑ Mexico

Where are Michelle and Antoine from?
❑ Japan ❑ Mexico ❑ France

Where are Rosa and Jose from?
❑ Mexico ❑ USA ❑ France

Where is Harry from?
❑ USA ❑ Mexico ❑ England

What language do they speak?

What language does Akiko speak?
_____

What language do Antoine and Michelle speak?
_____

What language does Harry speak?
_____

What language do Rosa and Jose speak?
_____

Spanish • English • French
Japanese

Complete the text with the words from the box below. In any order you like.

Friends from all around the world

We are friends from all over the world and we speak different languages.

_____ is from _____, he/she speaks _____.

_____ is from _____ and he/she speaks _____.

_____ are from _____, they speak _____.

_____ is from _____, she/he speaks _____.

_____ are from _____, they speak _____.

Where are you from? What language do you speak?

English • Spanish • Japanese • English • French • Japan • France • Mexico • USA • England • Harry • Tom • Rosa and Jose • Akiko • Michelle and Antoine

Write the words. Say them aloud

USA

England

Mexico

France

Japan

English

Spanish

French

Japanese

Countries, languages and nationalities

Country: France
Language: French
Nationality: French

Country: England
Language: English
Nationality: English

Country: USA
Language: English
Nationality: American

Country: Japan
Language: Japanese
Nationality: Japanes

Country: Mexico
Language: Spanish
Nationality: Mexican

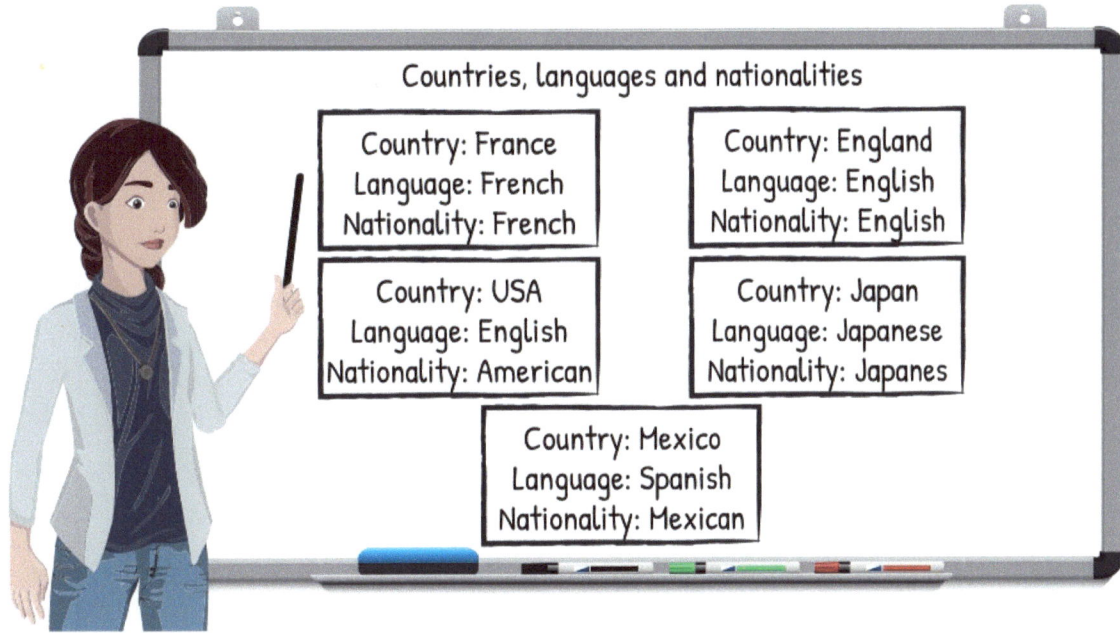

Answer the questions

What language does Akiko speak?

_____

Where is Akiko from?

_____

Where are Michelle and Antoine from?

_____

What language do they speak?

_____

Where is Harry from?

_____

What language does he speak?

_____

Find the language and country

Y	X	N	F	X	W	P	E	Z	P
B	Z	A	R	N	K	X	Q	P	M
E	F	P	E	N	G	L	I	S	H
S	F	A	N	E	C	A	B	D	S
E	M	J	C	V	T	R	F	S	I
N	E	M	H	M	T	M	R	V	N
A	X	O	M	G	R	S	A	M	A
P	I	D	N	A	L	G	N	E	P
A	C	H	I	F	A	Y	C	K	S
J	O	R	P	Y	S	T	E	W	I

ENGLAND   ENGLISH   JAPAN
MEXICO   SPANISH   USA
FRANCE   JAPANESE   FRENCH

How well did you do in this unit?

Write the CAN DO statement and assess yourself:

I can...

REFERENCES

• Communicative Language Learning. Retrieved August 23, 2019 from:
  http://www.educationbridge-id.com/news-a-article/72-communicative-language-teaching-clt.html
• Brown, H. Douglas (1994). Principles of Language Learning and Teaching. Prentice Hall.
• Beale, Jason (2008). Is communicative language teaching a thing of the past?. TESOL article.
• Harmer, Jeremy (2007). How to teach English. Pearson Longman.
• Richards, Jack C (2002). Methodology in Language Teaching. Cambridge University Press.
• Willis, Jane (1996). A Framework for Task-Based Learning. Longman.
• Hermitt, A. (2015). Spiral Learning, a superior approach? In Families.com. Retrieved January
  9th, 2015, from http://www.families.com/blog/spiral-learning-a-superior approach.
• Fleming, N. Baume, D. (2006) Learning Styles.
• Again: VARKing up the right tree! , Educational Developments, SEDA Ltd, Issue 7.4 Nov. 2006.
• Harmer, Jeremy. How to Teach English. Harlow: Longman, 1998. Krashen, Stephen D., and
  Terrell, Tracy D. The Natural Approach. Oxford: Pergamon, 1983.
• Sökmen, Anita J. "Current Trends in Teaching Second Language Vocabulary". In Vocabulary:
  Description, Acquisition and Pedagogy, edited by N. Schmitt and M. McCarthy, 237-257
  England: Cambridge University Press, 1997.
• Snow, Marguerite Ann. "Teaching English as a Second or Foreign Language". In Content-Based
  and Immersion Models for Second and Foreign Language Teaching" Edited by M. Celce-Murcia.
  Heinle & Heinle Thomson Learning, 2001.
• Roth, Genevieve. Teaching Very Young Children. Richmond Handbooks for English Teachers.
  London: Richmond Publishing. 1998.

ABOUT THE AUTHOR

Patricia Avila has been an English teacher for more than 45 years in her native Tijuana, B. C. She has a Bachelor's in Education from the National Pedagogical University (UPN).

Her experience as a teacher ranges from Kindergarten to Masters. She has functioned as coordinator of Bachelor's in ESL Teaching, as well as for various other universities; she has also worked as an Academic Consultant for different Publishing Houses for more than 15 years. Her wide experience and love for young learners has given her the opportunity to share with you **MY ENGLISH ZONE THE BOOK**, a series that will enhance the learning of English in a dynamic and fun way.